The Garden of Eden

retold by K.S. Rodriguez and Ellen Titlebaum
illustrated by Kallen Godsey

inchworm PRESS ™

In the beginning, God created heaven and earth. The earth had no shape, and darkness was everywhere. God said, "Let there be light!" And a burst of golden light brightened the sky.

God saw that light was good. God called the light Day and the darkness Night.

On the second day, God separated the sky from the waters below.

On the third day, land rose out of the waters and lush green plants grew on the land.

On the fourth day, God created the sun and the moon to separate day from night.

On the fifth day, God said, "Let the waters bring forth living creatures." Suddenly, the sea was bursting with fish and the land was full of animals.

On the sixth day, God created man. He called the man Adam and made him in His own image. God gave Adam thoughts and a spirit, which made him different from the other creatures.

And on the seventh day, God rested, because His work was done.

Adam woke up in the Garden of Eden. Around him were blossoming trees and bushes thick with leaves. He saw animals big and small playing nearby. He felt the warmth of the sun and the coolness of the waters.

Every color in the rainbow surrounded Adam. A peacock fanned its blue, purple, and turquoise feathers. A green and orange parrot perched on a limb near the deep blue stream.

Adam was happy in the beautiful garden. But something was missing. What was it?

Adam watched two birds make a nest. He spotted two fluffy rabbits playing near their burrow. Two deer nestled up to him. There were two of every kind of animal all around him.

Except for Adam. He was the only one of his kind.

God noticed Adam's loneliness. One night while Adam slept, God removed one of Adam's ribs. With that rib and some desert dust, God created woman.

The next morning, Adam woke up and saw Eve. He shared the garden's beauty with her, and they were happy. They picked berries and bathed in the waters, surrounded by trees bursting with delicious fruit.

God asked them to name the animals. They called the pudgy animal with large nostrils a Hippopotamus. They came across a spotted creature who could run like the wind and called it a Leopard. They decided the huge animal with the long gray trunk would be an Elephant.

One day, God spoke to Adam. "You must not eat from the Tree of Knowledge of Good and Evil," he said. "It is forbidden. If you do, you will feel shame and fear, and you will surely die."

Adam promised that he would never taste those fruits. He told Eve what God said and she too promised never to eat from the tree.

The days passed by happily in The Garden of Eden. Until the day the Serpent approached Eve. He charmed her and lured her to The Forbidden Tree of Knowledge of Good and Evil.

"You see that tree?" asked the Serpent.

"That's the forbidden tree!" cried Eve.

The Serpent laughed. "Forbidden tree?" he mimicked her. "That silver and gold tree with the finest fruit—the most succulent fruit a tree can bear —forbidden?" he scoffed. "Since when?"

"Since God told us never to eat from it," said Eve.

The Serpent laughed again. "Why would God say that? Maybe Adam wants to keep all that fine fruit to himself," added the Serpent slyly.

"You are so beautiful, Eve. You should be able to do anything you want," said the Serpent. Then he slithered up the tree, plucked a piece of fruit and took a big, juicy bite. The Serpent handed the fruit to Eve.

Eve studied the Serpent. He was still alive, and the fruit looked and smelled delicious. What harm could there be in taking a little bite?

Suddenly, she saw Adam running toward her. He was yelling and waving his arms. "Eve! Don't eat the fruit!" he cried.

But it was too late.

"Nothing happened to me, Adam," said Eve happily. "The Serpent and I have both tasted the fruit and we are just fine. Don't you want to try some?"

Adam saw that Eve was fine. He reached out and took the fruit from Eve's hand. Slowly, he bit into the sweet fruit.

Nothing would ever be the same in The Garden of Eden again.

Horrible thunder shook the land. Lightening raged across the sky. Terrified, Adam and Eve hid in the bushes. They were ashamed of their naked bodies and they shivered with fear.

"Adam! Eve!" God called. "Where are you? Did you eat from the Forbidden Tree?"

"Yes, God, we did," admitted Adam and Eve.

As the Serpent started to slip away, God shouted, "A curse on you, Serpent! You had no right to tempt them!" He turned back to Adam and Eve. "You must all face the consequences!" God warned.

God told Adam and Eve that they would now live with pain and sorrow, and they would have to toil long, hard days for their food. Worst of all, God ordered them to leave The Garden of Eden at once.

As they walked toward the gate, God spoke one last time. "I will never leave you," he promised. "But you will have to work much harder to keep close to me."

Adam and Eve took one last look at their beautiful garden and left, the heavy gate closing behind them forever.

They walked and walked through the desert until their skin burned from the hot sun, and their feet were full of blisters.

When they reached the land of Canaan, they built a mud hut and set up home. Soon they had a child, a baby boy named Cain. Two years later, they were blessed with another child named Abel.

As the boys grew older, Cain became envious of his brother. Cain thought that his parents loved Abel more. He even believed that God favored Abel!

One day, in a jealous rage, Cain killed Abel. Cain knew that killing his own brother was wrong. He knew that he would not escape the eye of God.

"Cain, where is your brother?" God asked.

"Am I my brother's keeper?" Cain answered.

"Yes!" God's angry voice boomed. "You know you are! Because you killed your brother you will wander homeless in the desert."

Cain was banished from Canaan just as his parents had been from The Garden of Eden.

Adam and Eve lived on without their sons. There was a sadness in their hearts.

After many years, God blessed them with another child, named Seth. From that day on Adam and Eve worked and prayed, hoping to one day return to their garden paradise.